The Book of Found Poetry

MZ Creates

Introduction

I am so excited to share this book with you. Within these pages are words from many many books. Pride and Prejudice, Emma, Jane Eyre, The Jungle Book, What Katy Did and so many more beloved classics.

If you haven't heard of found poetry yet you are in for a rare treat. While a simple google search will give you all you need to know and see. I want to give you a small introduction so that you can get started with this book immediately.

Found poetry is a poem that is 'found' among the words on a page. You can highlight the words you like to string them into a short poem. You can draw around them, paint around them and doodle too. This is an amazing exercise in creativity and fun and sometimes the poems that emerge are truly amazing!

A lot of artists and creatives have started doing this exercise to jumpstart their creativity or express their feelings.

This book has been crafted to make your found poetry journey fun and easy.

Each page is from a different book and is printed on one side and left blank on the other. This is so that you can tear out the pages you want to put into your art journal or display in your planner or in other mixed media pieces. You can also just leave them in the book and turn this into your found poetry journal.

Check out my YouTube channel MZ Creates and just search for The Book of Found Poetry to see videos of my experiments. I really hope you have fun playing with these pages and finding meaning in these words!

MZ

CHAPTER X

The appearance of the little sitting-room as they entered, was tranquility itself; Mrs. Bates, deprived of her usual employment, slumbering on one side of the fire, Frank Churchill, at a table near her, most deedily occupied about her spectacles, and Jane Fairfax, standing with her back to them, intent on her pianoforte. Busy as he was, however, the young man was yet able to shew a most happy countenance on seeing Emma again. "This is a pleasure," said he, in rather a low voice, "coming at least ten minutes earlier than I had calculated. You find me trying to be useful; tell me if you think I shall succeed." "What!" said Mrs. Weston, "have not you finished it yet? you would not earn a very good livelihood as a working silversmith at this rate." "I have not been working uninterruptedly," he replied, "I have been assisting Miss Fairfax in trying to make her instrument stand steadily, it was not quite firm; an unevenness in the floor, I believe. You see we have been wedging one leg with paper. This was very kind of you to be persuaded to come. I was almost afraid you would be hurrying home." He contrived that she should be seated by him; and was sufficiently employed in looking out the best baked apple for her, and trying to make her help or advise him in his work, till Jane Fairfax was quite ready to sit down to the pianoforte again. That she was not immediately ready, Emma did suspect to arise from the state of her nerves; she had not yet possessed the instrument long enough to touch it without emotion; she must reason herself into the power of performance; and Emma could not but pity such feelings, whatever their origin, and could not but resolve never to expose them to her neighbour again. At last Jane began, and though the first bars were feebly given, the powers of the instrument were gradually done full justice to. Mrs. Weston had been delighted before, and was delighted again; Emma joined her in all her praise; and the pianoforte, with every proper discrimination, was pronounced to be altogether of the highest promise. "Whoever Colonel Campbell might employ," said Frank

with it." "You are expecting her again, you say, this morning?" "Almost every moment. She has been gone longer already than she intended." "Something has happened to delay her; some visitors perhaps." "Highbury gossips!-- Tiresome wretches!" "Harriet may not consider everybody tiresome that you would." Emma knew this was too true for contradiction, and therefore said nothing. He presently added, with a smile, "I do not pretend to fix on times or places, but I must tell you that I have good reason to believe your little friend will soon hear of something to her advantage." "Indeed! how so? of what sort?" "A very serious sort, I assure you;" still smiling. "Very serious! I can think of but one thing--Who is in love with her? Who makes you their confidant?" Emma was more than half in hopes of Mr. Elton's having dropped a hint. Mr. Knightley was a sort of general friend and adviser, and she knew Mr. Elton looked up to him. "I have reason to think," he replied, "that Harriet Smith will soon have an offer of marriage, and from a most unexceptionable quarter:--Robert Martin is the man. Her visit to Abbey-Mill, this summer, seems to have done his business. He is desperately in love and means to marry her." "He is very obliging," said Emma; "but is he sure that Harriet means to marry him?" "Well, well, means to make her an offer then. Will that do? He came to the Abbey two evenings ago, on purpose to consult me about it. He knows I have a thorough regard for him and all his family, and, I believe, considers me as one of his best friends. He came to ask me whether I thought it would be imprudent in him to settle so early; whether I thought her too young: in short, whether I approved his choice altogether; having some apprehension perhaps of her being considered (especially since your making so much of her) as in a line of society above him. I was very much pleased with all that he said. I never hear better sense from any one than Robert Martin. He always speaks to the purpose; open, straightforward, and very well judging. He told me everything; his circumstances and plans, and what they all proposed doing in the event of his marriage. He is an excellent young man, both as son and brother. I had no hesitation in advising him to marry. He proved to me that he could afford it; and that being the case, I was convinced he could not do better. I praised the fair lady too, and altogether sent him away very happy. If he had never esteemed my opinion before, he would have thought highly of me then; and, I dare say, left the house thinking me

surprised that he should have fallen in love." "Oh! no--there is nothing to surprise one at all.--A pretty fortune; and she came in his way." "I dare say," returned Harriet, sighing again, "I dare say she was very much attached to him." "Perhaps she might; but it is not every man's fate to marry the woman who loves him best. Miss Hawkins perhaps wanted a home, and thought this the best offer she was likely to have." "Yes," said Harriet earnestly, "and well she might, nobody could ever have a better. Well, I wish them happy with all my heart. And now, Miss Woodhouse, I do not think I shall mind seeing them again. He is just as superior as ever;--but being married, you know, it is quite a different thing. No, indeed, Miss Woodhouse, you need not be afraid; I can sit and admire him now without any great misery. To know that he has not thrown himself away, is such a comfort!--She does seem a charming young woman, just what he deserves. Happy creature! He called her 'Augusta.' How delightful!" When the visit was returned, Emma made up her mind. She could then see more and judge better. From Harriet's happening not to be at Hartfield, and her father's being present to engage Mr. Elton, she had a quarter of an hour of the lady's conversation to herself, and could composedly attend to her; and the quarter of an hour quite convinced her that Mrs. Elton was a vain woman, extremely well satisfied with herself, and thinking much of her own importance; that she meant to shine and be very superior, but with manners which had been formed in a bad school, pert and familiar; that all her notions were drawn from one set of people, and one style of living; that if not foolish she was ignorant, and that her society would certainly do Mr. Elton no good. Harriet would have been a better match. If not wise or refined herself, she would have connected him with those who were; but Miss Hawkins, it might be fairly supposed from her easy conceit, had been the best of her own set. The rich brother-in-law near Bristol was the pride of the alliance, and his place and his carriages were the pride of him. The very first subject after being seated was Maple Grove, "My brother Mr. Suckling's seat;"--a comparison of Hartfield to Maple Grove. The grounds of Hartfield were small, but neat and pretty; and the house was modern and well-built. Mrs. Elton seemed most favourably impressed by the size of the room, the entrance, and all that she could see or imagine. "Very like Maple Grove indeed!--She was quite struck by the likeness!--That room was the very shape

CHAPTER I

It is a truth universally acknowledged, that a single man in possession of a good fortune, must be in want of a wife. However, little known the feelings or views of such a man may be on his first entering a neighbourhood, this truth is so well fixed in the minds of the surrounding families, that he is considered the rightful property of someone or other of their daughters. "My dear Mr. Bennet," said his lady to him one day, "have you heard that Netherfield Park is let at last?" Mr. Bennet replied that he had not. "But it is," returned she; "for Mrs. Long has just been here, and she told me all about it." Mr. Bennet made no answer. "Do you not want to know who has taken it?" cried his wife impatiently. " You want to tell me, and I have no objection to hearing it." This was invitation enough. "Why, my dear, you must know, Mrs. Long says that Netherfield is taken by a young man of large fortune from the north of England; that he came down on Monday in a chaise and four to see the place, and was so much delighted with it, that he agreed with Mr. Morris immediately; that he is to take possession before Michaelmas, and some of his servants are to be in the house by the end of next week." "What is his name?" "Bingley." "Is he married or single?" "Oh! Single, my dear, to be sure! A single man of large fortune; four or five thousand a year. What a fine thing for our girls!" "How so? How can it affect them?" "My dear Mr. Bennet," replied his wife, "how can you be so tiresome! You must know that I am thinking of his marrying one of them." "Is that his design in settling here?" "Design! Nonsense, how can you talk so! But it is very likely that he may fall in love with one of them, and therefore you must visit him as soon as he comes." "I see no occasion for that. You and the girls may go, or you may send them by themselves, which perhaps will be still better, for as you are as handsome as any of them, Mr. Bingley may like you the best of the party." "My dear, you flatter me. I certainly have had my share of beauty, but I do not pretend to be anything extraordinary now. When a woman has five grown-up daughters, she ought to give over thinking of her own beauty." "In

her utter amazement, she saw Mr. Darcy walk into the room. In a hurried manner he immediately began an inquiry after her health, imputing his visit to a wish of hearing that she were better. She answered him with cold civility. He sat down for a few moments, and then getting up, walked about the room. Elizabeth was surprised, but said not a word. After a silence of several minutes, he came towards her in an agitated manner, and thus began: "In vain I have struggled. It will not do. My feelings will not be repressed. You must allow me to tell you how ardently I admire and love you." Elizabeth's astonishment was beyond expression. She stared, coloured, doubted, and was silent. This he considered sufficient encouragement; and the avowal of all that he felt, and had long felt for her, immediately followed. He spoke well; but there were feelings besides those of the heart to be detailed; and he was not more eloquent on the subject of tenderness than of pride. His sense of her inferiority--of its being a degradation--of the family obstacles which had always opposed to inclination, were dwelt on with a warmth which seemed due to the consequence he was wounding, but was very unlikely to recommend his suit. In spite of her deeply-rooted dislike, she could not be insensible to the compliment of such a man's affection, and though her intentions did not vary for an instant, she was at first sorry for the pain he was to receive; till, roused to resentment by his subsequent language, she lost all compassion in anger. She tried, however, to compose herself to answer him with patience, when he should have done. He concluded with representing to her the strength of that attachment which, in spite of all his endeavours, he had found impossible to conquer; and with expressing his hope that it would now be rewarded by her acceptance of his hand. As he said this, she could easily see that he had no doubt of a favourable answer. He spoke of apprehension and anxiety, but his countenance expressed real security. Such a circumstance could only exasperate your family owe me nothing. Much as I respect them, I believe I thought only of you ." Elizabeth was too much embarrassed to say a word. After a short pause, her companion added, "You are too

generous to trifle with me. If your feelings are still what they were last April, tell me so at once. My affections and wishes are unchanged, but one word from you will silence me on this subject forever." Elizabeth, feeling all the more than common awkwardness and anxiety of his situation, now forced herself to speak; and immediately, though not very fluently, gave him to understand that her sentiments had undergone so material a change, since the period to which he alluded, as to make her receive with gratitude and pleasure his present assurances. The happiness which this reply produced, was such as he had probably never felt before; and he expressed himself on the occasion as sensibly and as warmly as a man violently in love can be supposed to do. Had Elizabeth been able to encounter his eye, she might have seen how well the expression of heartfelt delight, diffused over his face, became him; but, though she could not look, she could listen, and he told her of feelings, which, in proving of what importance she was to him, made his affection every moment more valuable. They walked on, without knowing in what direction. There was too much to be thought, and felt, and said, for attention to any other objects. She soon learnt that they were indebted for their present good understanding to the efforts of his aunt, who did call on him in her return through London, and there relate her journey to Longbourn, its motive, and the substance of her conversation with Elizabeth; dwelling emphatically on every expression of the latter which, in her ladyship's apprehension, peculiarly denoted her perverseness and assurance; in the belief that such a relation must assist her endeavours to obtain that promise from her nephew which she had refused to give. But, unluckily for her ladyship, its effect had been exactly contrariwise. "It taught me to hope," said he, "as I had scarcely ever allowed myself to hope before. I knew enough of your disposition to be certain that, had you been absolutely, irrevocably decided against me, you would have acknowledged it to Lady

1 DOWN THE RABBIT HOLE

Alice was beginning to get very tired of sitting by her sister on the bank, and of having nothing to do: once or twice she had peeped into the book her sister was reading, but it had no pictures or conversations in it, `and what is the use of a book,' thought Alice `without pictures or conversation?'

So she was considering in her own mind (as well as she could, for the hot day made her feel very sleepy and stupid), whether the pleasure of making a daisy-chain would be worth the trouble of getting up and picking the daisies, when suddenly a White Rabbit with pink eyes ran close by her.

There was nothing so *very* remarkable in that; nor did Alice think it so *very* much out of the way to hear the Rabbit say to itself, `Oh dear! Oh dear! I shall be late!' (when she thought it over afterwards, it occurred to her that she ought to have wondered at this, but at the time it all seemed quite natural); but when the Rabbit actually *took a watch out of its waistcoat-pocket*, and looked at it, and then hurried on, Alice started to her feet, for it flashed across her mind that she had never before seen a rabbit with either a waistcoat-pocket, or a watch to take out of it, and burning with curiosity, she ran across the field after it, and fortunately was just in time to see it pop down a large rabbit-hole under the hedge.

In another moment down went Alice after it, never once considering how in the world she was to get out again.

The rabbit-hole went straight on like a tunnel for some way, and then dipped suddenly down, so suddenly that Alice had not a moment to think about stopping herself before she found herself falling down a very deep well.

Either the well was very deep, or she fell very slowly, for she had plenty of time as she went down to look about her and to wonder what was going to happen next. First, she tried to look down and make out what she was coming to, but it was too dark to see anything; then she looked at the sides of the well, and noticed that they were filled with cupboards and book-shelves; here and there she saw maps and pictures hung upon pegs. She took down a jar from one of the shelves as she passed; it was labelled `ORANGE MARMALADE', but to her great disappointment it was empty: she did not like to drop the jar for fear of killing somebody, so managed to put it into one of the cupboards as she fell past it.

`Well!' thought Alice to herself, `after such a fall as this, I shall think nothing of tumbling downstairs! How brave they'll all think me at home! Why, I wouldn't say anything about it, even if I fell off the top of the house!' (Which was very likely true.)

Down, down, down. Would the fall *never* come to an end! `I wonder how many miles I've fallen by this time?' she said aloud. `I must be getting somewhere near the centre of the earth. Let me see: that would be four thousand miles down, I think--' (for, you see, Alice had learnt several things of this sort in her lessons in the schoolroom, and though this was not a *very* good opportunity for showing off her knowledge, as there was no one to listen to her, still it was good practice to say it over) `--yes, that's about the right distance--but then I wonder what Latitude or Longitude I've got to?' (Alice had no idea what Latitude was, or Longitude either, but thought they were nice grand words to say.)

`What a curious feeling!' said Alice; `I must be shutting up like a telescope.'

And so it was indeed: she was now only ten inches high, and her face brightened up at the thought that she was now the right size for going through the little door into that lovely garden. First, however, she waited for a few minutes to see if she was going to shrink any further: she felt a little nervous about this; `for it might end, you know,' said Alice to herself, `in my going out altogether, like a candle. I wonder what I should be like then?' And she tried to fancy what the flame of a candle is like after the candle is blown out, for she could not remember ever having seen such a thing.

After a while, finding that nothing more happened, she decided on going into the garden at once; but, alas for poor Alice! when she got to the door, she found she had forgotten the little golden key, and when she went back to the table for it, she found she could not possibly reach it: she could see it quite plainly through the glass, and she tried her best to climb up one of the legs of the table, but it was too slippery; and when she had tired herself out with trying, the poor little thing sat down and cried.

`Come, there's no use in crying like that!' said Alice to herself, rather sharply; `I advise you to leave off this minute!' She generally gave herself very good advice, (though she very seldom followed it), and sometimes she scolded herself so severely as to bring tears into her eyes; and once she remembered trying to box her own ears for having cheated herself in a game of croquet she was playing against herself, for this curious child was very fond of pretending to be two people. `But it's no use now,'

`I'm sure I'm not Ada,' she said, `for her hair goes in such long ringlets, and mine doesn't go in ringlets at all; and I'm

sure I can't be Mabel, for I know all sorts of things, and she, oh! she knows such a very little! Besides, *she's* she, and I'm I, and--oh dear, how puzzling it all is! I'll try if I know all the things I used to know. Let me see: four times five is twelve, and four times six is thirteen, and four times seven is--oh dear! I shall never get to twenty at that rate! However, the Multiplication Table doesn't signify: let's try Geography. London is the capital of Paris, and Paris is the capital of Rome, and Rome--no, *that's* all wrong, I'm certain! I must have been changed for Mabel! I'll try and say "How doth the little--"' and she crossed her hands on her lap as if she were saying lessons, and began to repeat it, but her voice sounded hoarse and strange, and the words did not come the same as they used to do:--

```
`How doth the little crocodile
  Improve his shining tail,
And pour the waters of the Nile
  On every golden scale!

`How cheerfully he seems to grin,
  How neatly spread his claws,
And welcome little fishes in
  With gently smiling jaws!'
```

`I'm sure those are not the right words,' said poor Alice, and her eyes filled with tears again as she went on, `I must be Mabel after all, and I shall have to go and live in that poky little house, and have next to no toys to play with, and oh! ever so many lessons to learn! No, I've made up my mind about it; if I'm Mabel, I'll stay down here! It'll be no use their putting their heads down and saying "Come up again, dear!" I shall only look up and say "Who am I then? Tell me that first, and then, if I like being that person, I'll come up: if not, I'll stay down here till I'm somebody else"--but, oh dear!' cried Alice, with a sudden burst of tears, `I do

wish they *would* put their heads down! I am so *very* tired of being all alone here!'

As she said this she looked down at her hands, and was surprised to see that she had put on one of the Rabbit's little white kid gloves while she was talking. `How *can* I have done that?' she thought. `I must be growing small again.' She got up and went to the table to measure herself by it, and found that, as nearly as she could guess, she was now about two feet high, and was going on shrinking rapidly: she soon found out that the cause of this was the fan she was holding, and she dropped it hastily, just in time to avoid shrinking away altogether.

`That *was* a narrow escape!' said Alice, a good deal frightened at the sudden change, but very glad to find herself still in existence; `and now for the garden!' and she ran with all speed back to the little door: but, alas! the little door was shut again, and the little golden key was lying on the glass table as before, `and things are worse than ever,' thought the poor child, `for I never was so small as this before, never! And I declare it's too bad, that it is!'

As she said these words her foot slipped, and in another moment, splash! she was up to her chin in salt water. Her first idea was that she had somehow fallen into the sea, `and in that case I can go back by railway,' she said to herself. (Alice had been to the seaside once in her life, and had come to the general conclusion, that wherever you go to on the English coast you find a number of bathing machines in the sea, some children digging in the sand with wooden spades, then a row of lodging houses, and behind them a railway station.) However, she soon made out that

KATY'S name was Katy Carr. She lived in the town of Burnet, which wasn't a very big town, but was growing as fast as it knew how. The house she lived in stood on the edge of town. It was a large square house, white, with green blinds, and had a porch in front, over which roses and clematis made a thick bower. Four tall locust trees shaded the gravel path which led to the front gate. On one side of the house was an orchard; on the other side were wood piles and barns, and an ice-house. Behind was a kitchen garden sloping to the south; and behind that a pasture with a brook in it, and butternut trees, and four cows – two red ones, a yellow one with sharp horns tipped with tin, and a dear little white one named Daisy.

There were six of the Carr children – four girls and two boys. Katy, the oldest, was twelve years old; little Phil, the youngest, was four, and the rest fitted in between.

Dr. Carr, their Papa, was a dear, kind, busy man, who was away from home all day, and sometimes all night too, taking care of sick people. The children hadn't any Mamma. She had died when Phil was a baby, four years before my story began. Katy could remember her pretty well; to the rest she was but a sad, sweet name, spoken on Sunday, and at prayer-times, or when Papa was specially gentle and solemn.

In place of this Mamma, whom they recollected so dimly, there was Aunt Izzie, Papa's sister, who came to take care of them when Mamma went away on that long journey, from which, for so many months, the little ones kept hoping she might return. Aunt Izzie was a small woman, sharp-faced and thin, rather old-looking, and very neat and particular about everything. She meant to be kind to the children, but they puzzled her much, because they were not a bit like herself when she was a child. Aunt Izzie had been a gentle, tidy little thing, who loved to sit as Curly Locks did, sewing long seams in the parlor, and to have her head patted by older people, and be told that she was a good girl; whereas Katy tore her dress every day, hated sewing, and didn't care a button about being called "good," while Clover and Elsie shied off like restless ponies when anyone tried to pat their heads. It was very perplexing to Aunt Izzie, and she found it quite hard to forgive the children for being so "unaccountable," and so little like the good boys and girls in Sunday-school memoirs, who were the young people she liked best, and understood most about.

Then Dr. Carr was another person who worried her. He wished to have the children hardy and bold, and encouraged climbing and rough plays, in spite of the bumps and ragged clothes which resulted. In fact, there was just one half-hour of the day when Aunt Izzie was really satisfied about her charges, and that was the half-hour before breakfast, when she had made a law that they were all to sit in their little chairs and learn the Bible verse for the day. At this time she looked at them with pleased eyes, they were all so spick and span, with such nicely-brushed jackets and such neatly-combed hair. But the moment the bell rang her comfort was over. From that time on, they were what she called "not fit to be seen." The neighbors pitied her very much. They used to count the sixty stiff white pantalette legs hung out to dry every Monday morning, and say to each other what a sight of washing those children made, and what a chore it must be for poor Miss Carr to keep them so nice. But poor Miss Carr didn't think them at all nice; that was the worst of it.

"Clover, go up stairs and wash your hands! Dorry, pick your hat off the floor and hang it on the nail! Not that nail – the third nail from the corner!" These were the kind of things Aunt Izzie was saying all day long. The children minded her pretty well, but they didn't exactly love her, I fear. They called her "Aunt Izzie" always, never "Aunty." Boys and girls will know what *that* meant.

I want to show you the little Carrs, and I don't know that I could ever have a better chance than one day when five out of the six were perched on top of the ice-house, like chickens on a roost. This ice-house was one of their favorite places. It was only a low roof set over a hole in the ground, and, as it stood in the middle of the side-yard, it always seemed to the children that the shortest road to every place was up one of its slopes and down the other. They also liked to mount to the ridge-pole, and then, still keeping the sitting position, to let go, and scrape slowly down over the warm shingles to the ground. It was bad for their shoes and trousers, of course; but what of that? Shoes and trousers, and clothes generally, were Aunt Izzie's affair; theirs was to slide and enjoy themselves.

Clover, next in age to Katy, sat in the middle. She was a fair, sweet dumpling of a girl, with thick pig-tails of light brown hair, and short-sighted blue eyes, which seemed to hold tears, just ready to fall from under the blue. Really, Clover was the jolliest little thing in the world; but these eyes, and her soft cooing voice, always made people feel like petting her and taking her part. Once, when she was very small, she ran

Miss Miller's clock was about four minutes slower than Mrs. Knight's, so the next play-ground was empty. It was a warm, breezy day, and as Katy sat there, suddenly a gust of wind came, and seizing her sun-bonnet, which was only half tied on, whirled it across the roof. She clutched after it as it flew, but too late. Once, twice, thrice, it flapped, then it disappeared over the edge, and Katy, flying after, saw it lying a crumpled lilac heap in the very middle of the enemy's yard.

This was horrible! Not merely losing the bonnet, for Katy was comfortably indifferent as to what became of her clothes, but to lose it *so*. In another minute the Miller girls would be out. Already she seemed to see them dancing war-dances round the unfortunate bonnet, pinning it on a pole, using it as a foot-ball, waving it over the fence, and otherwise treating it as Indians treat a captive taken in war. Was it to be endured? Never! Better die first! And with very much the feeling of a person who faces destruction rather than forfeit honour, Katy set her teeth, and, sliding rapidly down the roof, seized the fence, and with one bold leap vaulted into Miss Miller's yard.

Just then the recess bell tinkled; and a little Millerite who sat by the window, and who, for two seconds, had been dying to give the exciting information, squeaked out to the others: "There's Katy Carr in our back-yard!"

Out poured the Millerites, big and little. Their wrath and indignation at this daring invasion cannot be described. With a howl of fury they precipitated themselves upon Katy, but she was quick as they, and holding the rescued bonnet in her hand, was already half-way up the fence.

There are moments when it is a fine thing to be tall. On this occasion Katy's long legs and arms served her an excellent turn. Nothing but a Daddy Long Legs ever climbed so fast or so wildly as she did now. In one second she had gained the top of the fence. Just as she went over a Millerite seized her by the last foot, and almost dragged her boot off.

Wherever Miss Petingill went all sorts of treasures went with her. The children liked to have her come, for it was as good as a fairy story, or the circus, to see her things unpacked. Miss Petingill was very much afraid of burglars; she lay awake half the night listening for them, and nothing on earth would have persuaded her to go anywhere, leaving behind what she called her "Plate." This stately word meant six old tea-spoons, very thin and bright and sharp, and a butter-knife, whose handle set forth that it was "A testimonial of gratitude, for saving the life of Ithuriel Jobson, aged seven, on the occasion of his being attacked with quinsy sore throat." Miss Petingill was very proud of her knife. It and the spoons travelled about in a little basket which hung on her arm, and was never allowed to be out of her sight, even when the family she was sewing for were the honestest people in the world.

Then, beside the plate-basket, Miss Petingill never stirred without Tom, her tortoise-shell cat. Tom was a beauty, and knew his power; he ruled Miss Petingill with a rod of iron, and always sat in the rocking-chair when there was one. It was no matter where *she* sat, Miss Petingill told people, but Tom was delicate, and must be made comfortable. A big family Bible always came too, and a special red merino pin-cushion, and some "shade pictures" of old Mr. and Mrs. Petingill and Peter Petingill, who was drowned at sea; and photographs of Mrs. Porter, who used to be Marcia Petingill, and Mrs. Porter's husband, and all the Porter children. Many little boxes and jars came also, and a long row of phials and bottles, filled with home-made physic and herb teas. Miss Petingill could not have slept without having them beside her, for, as she said, how did she know that she might not be "took sudden" with something, and die for want of a little ginger-balsam or pennyroyal?

The Carr children always made so much noise, that it required something unusual to make Miss Petingill drop her work, as she did now, and fly to the window. In fact there *was* a tremendous hubbub: hurrahs from Dorry, stamping of feet, and a great outcry of shrill, glad voices. Looking down, Miss Petingill saw the whole six – no seven, for Cecy was there too – stream out of the wood-house door – which wasn't a door, but only a tall open arch – and rush noisily across the yard. Katy was at the head, bearing a large black bottle

CHAPTER X.

ST. NICHOLAS AND ST. VALENTINE.

WHAT are the children all doing to-day?" said Katy, laying down "Norway and the Norwegians," which she was reading for the fourth time; "I haven't seen them since breakfast."

Aunt Izzie, who was sewing on the other side of the room, looked up from her work.

"I don't know," she said; "they're over at Cecy's, or somewhere. They'll be back before long, I guess."

Her voice sounded a little odd and mysterious, but Katy didn't notice it.

"I thought of such a nice plan yesterday," she went on. "That was that all of them should hang their stockings up here to-morrow night instead of in the nursery. Then I could see them open their presents, you know. Mayn't they, Aunt Izzie? It would be real fun."

"I don't believe there will be any objection," replied her aunt. She looked as if she were trying not to laugh. Katy wondered what *was* the matter with her.

It was more than two months now since Cousin Helen went away, and Winter had fairly come. Snow was falling out-doors. Katy could see the thick flakes go whirling past the window, but the sight did not chill her. It only made the room look warmer and more cosy. It was a pleasant room now. There was a bright fire in the grate. Everything was neat and orderly, the air was sweet with mignonette, from a little glass of flowers which stood on the table, and the Katy who lay in bed, was a very different-looking Katy from the forlorn girl of the last chapter.

Cousin Helen's visit, though it lasted only one day, did great good. Not that Katy grew perfect all at once. None of us do that, even in books. But

'Mamma will come directly, Miss Hale. She desired me to apologise to you as it is. Perhaps you know my brother has imported hands from Ireland, and it has irritated the Milton people excessively--as if he hadn't a right to get labour where he could; and the stupid wretches here wouldn't work for him; and now they've frightened these poor Irish starvelings so with their threats, that we daren't let them out. You may see them huddled in that top room in the mill,--and they're to sleep there, to keep them safe from those brutes, who will neither work nor let them work. And mamma is seeing about their food, and John is speaking to them, for some of the women are crying to go back. Ah! here's mamma!'

Mrs. Thornton came in with a look of black sternness on her face, which made Margaret feel she had arrived at a bad time to trouble her with her request. However, it was only in compliance with Mrs. Thornton's expressed desire, that she would ask for whatever they might want in the progress of her mother's illness. Mrs. Thornton's brow contracted, and her mouth grew set, while Margaret spoke with gentle modesty of her mother's restlessness, and Dr. Donaldson's wish that she should have the relief of a water-bed. She ceased. Mrs. Thornton did not reply immediately. Then she started up and exclaimed--

'They're at the gates! Call John, Fanny,--call him in from the mill! They're at the gates! They'll batter them in! Call John, I say!'

And simultaneously, the gathering tramp--to which she had been listening, instead of heeding Margaret's words--was heard just right outside the wall, and an increasing din of angry voices raged behind the wooden barrier, which shook as if the unseen maddened crowd made battering-rams of their bodies, and retreated a short space only to come with more united steady impetus against it, till their great beats made the strong gates quiver, like reeds before the wind. The women gathered round the windows, fascinated to look on the scene which terrified them. Mrs. Thornton, the women-servants, Margaret,--all were there. Fanny had returned, screaming up-stairs as if pursued at every step, and had thrown herself in hysterical sobbing on the sofa. Mrs. Thornton watched for her son, who was still in the mill. He came out, looked up at them--the pale cluster of faces--and smiled good courage to them, before he locked the factory-door. Then he called to one of the women to come down and undo his own door, which Fanny had fastened behind her in her mad flight. Mrs. Thornton herself went. And the sound of his well-known and commanding voice, seemed to have been like the taste of blood to the infuriated multitude outside. Hitherto they had been voiceless, wordless, needing all their breath for their hard-labouring efforts to break down the gates. But now, hearing him speak

"Why, of course they're not ripe!" said Clover, putting one into her mouth. "Can't you tell by the taste? They're as green as can be."

"I don't care, if Katy says they're ripe I shall eat 'em," answered Phil, defiantly, marching into the house.

"What did Philly want?" asked Elsie, opening the parlor door as Phil went up stairs.

"Only to know if the currants are ripe enough to eat."

"How particular he always is about asking now!" said Elsie; "he's afraid of another dose of salts."

"I should think he would be," replied Clover, laughing. "Johnnie says she never was so scared in her life as when Papa called them, and they looked up, and saw him standing there with the bottle in one hand and a spoon in the other!"

"Yes," went on Elsie, "and you know Dorry held his in his mouth for ever so long, and then went round the corner of the house and spat it out! Papa said he had a good mind to make him take another spoonful, but he remembered that after all Dorry had the bad taste a great deal longer than the others, so he didn't. I think it was an *awful* punishment, don't you?"

"Yes, but it was a good one, for none of them have ever touched green gooseberries since. Have you got through practising? It doesn't seem like an hour yet."

"Oh, it isn't – it's only twenty-five minutes. But Katy told me not to sit more than half an hour at a time without getting up and running round to rest. I'm going to walk twice down to the gate, and twice back. I promised her I would." And Elsie set off, clapping her hands briskly before and behind her as she walked.

"Why – what is Bridget doing in Papa's room?" she asked, as she came back the second time. "She's flapping things out of the window. Are the girls up there? I thought they were cleaning the dining-room."

"They're doing both. Katy said it was such a good chance, having Papa away, that she would have both the carpets taken up at once. There isn't

going to be any dinner to-day, only just bread and butter, and milk, and cold ham, up in Katy's room, because Debby is helping too, so as to get through and save Papa all the fuss. And see," exhibiting her sewing, "Katy's making a new cover for Papa's pincushion, and I'm hemming the ruffle to go round it."

"How nicely you hem!" said Elsie. "I wish I had something for Papa's room too. There's my washstand mats – but the one for the soap-dish isn't finished. Do you suppose, if Katy would excuse me from the rest of my practising, I could get it done? I've a great mind to go and ask her."

"There's her bell!" said Clover, as a little tinkle sounded up stairs; "I'll ask her if you like."

"No, let me go. I'll see what she wants." But Clover was already half-way across the hall, and the two girls ran up side by side. There was often a little strife between them as to which should answer Katy's bell. Both liked to wait on her so much.

Katy came to meet them as they entered. Not on her feet: that, alas! was still only a far-off possibility; but in a chair with large wheels, with which she was rolling herself across the room. This chair was a great comfort to her. Sitting in it, she could get to her closet and her bureau-drawers, and help herself to what she wanted without troubling anybody. It was only lately that she had been able to use it. Dr. Carr considered her doing so as a hopeful sign, but he had never told Katy this. She had grown accustomed to her invalid life at last, and was cheerful in it, and he thought it unwise to make her restless, by exciting hopes which might after all end in fresh disappointment.

She met the girls with a bright smile as they came in, and said:

"Oh, Clovy, it was you I rang for! I am troubled for fear Bridget will meddle with the things on Papa's table.

'Be sure and take good care of her,' cried she to the guard, as he lifted me into the inside. 'Ay, ay!' was the answer: the door was slapped to, a voice exclaimed 'All right,' and on we drove. Thus was I severed from Bessie and Gateshead; thus whirled away to unknown, and, as I then deemed, remote and mysterious regions. I remember but little of the journey; I only know that the day seemed to me of a preternatural length, and that we appeared to travel over hundreds of miles of road. We passed through several towns, and in one, a very large one, the coach stopped; the horses were taken out, and the passengers alighted to dine. I was carried into an inn, where the guard wanted me to have some dinner; but, as I had no appetite, he left me in an immense room with a fireplace at each end, a chandelier pendent from the ceiling, and a little red gallery high up against the wall filled with musical instruments. Here I walked about for a long time, feeling very strange, and mortally apprehensive of some one coming in and kidnapping me; for I believed in kidnappers, their exploits having frequently figured in Bessie's fireside chronicles. At last the guard returned; once more I was stowed away in the coach, my protector mounted his own seat, sounded his hollow horn, and away we rattled over the 'stony street' of L-. The afternoon came on wet and somewhat misty: as it waned into dusk, I began to feel that we were getting very far indeed from Gateshead: we ceased to pass through towns; the country changed; great grey hills heaved up round the horizon: as twilight deepened, we descended a valley, dark with wood, and long after night had overclouded the prospect, I heard a wild wind rushing amongst trees. Lulled by the sound, I at last dropped asleep; I had not long slumbered when the sudden cessation of motion awoke me; the coach- door was open, and a person like a servant was standing at it: I saw her face and dress by the light of the lamps. 'Is there a little girl called Jane Eyre here?' she asked. I answered 'Yes,' and was then lifted out; my trunk was handed down, and the coach instantly drove away. I was stiff with long sitting, and bewildered with the noise and motion of the coach: Gathering my faculties, I looked about me. Rain, wind, and darkness filled the air; nevertheless, I dimly discerned a wall before me and a door open in it; through this door I passed with my new guide: she shut and locked it behind her. There was now visible a house or houses—for the building spread far—with many windows, and lights burning in some; we went up a broad pebbly path, splashing wet, and

home that night, Jane, though probably you were not aware that I thought of you or watched for you. The next day I observed you—myself unseen—for half-an-hour, while you played with Adele in the gallery. It was a snowy day, I recollect, and you could not go out of doors. I was in my room; the door was ajar: I could both listen and watch. Adele claimed your outward attention for a while; yet I fancied your thoughts were elsewhere: but you were very patient with her, my little Jane; you talked to her and amused her a long time. When at last she left you, you lapsed at once into deep reverie: you betook yourself slowly to pace the gallery. Now and then, in passing a casement, you glanced out at the thick-falling snow; you listened to the sobbing wind, and again you paced gently on and dreamed. I think those day visions were not dark: there was a pleasurable illumination in your eye occasionally, a soft excitement in your aspect, which told of no bitter, bilious, hypochondriac brooding: your look revealed rather the sweet musings of youth when its spirit follows on willing wings the flight of Hope up and on to an ideal heaven. The voice of Mrs. Fairfax, speaking to a servant in the hall, wakened you: and how curiously you smiled to and at yourself, Janet! There was much sense in your smile: it was very shrewd, and seemed to make light of your own abstraction. It seemed to say—'My fine visions are all very well, but I must not forget they are absolutely unreal. I have a rosy sky and a green flowery Eden in my brain; but without, I am perfectly aware, lies at my feet a rough tract to travel, and around me gather black tempests to encounter.' You ran downstairs and demanded of Mrs. Fairfax some occupation: the weekly house accounts to make up, or something of that sort, I think it was. I was vexed with you for getting out of my sight. 'Impatiently I waited for evening, when I might summon you to my presence. An unusual—to me—a perfectly new character I suspected was yours: I desired to search it deeper and know it better. You entered the room with a look and air at once shy and independent: you were quaintly dressed—much as you are now. I made you talk: ere long I found you full of strange contrasts. Your garb and manner were restricted by rule; your air was often diffident, and altogether that of one refined by nature, but absolutely unused to society, and a good deal afraid of making herself disadvantageously conspicuous by some solecism or blunder; yet when addressed, you lifted a keen, a daring, and a glowing eye to your interlocutor's face: there was penetration

CHAPTER IX WHICH TELLS OF THE MAN

It rained the next time Pollyanna saw the Man. She greeted him, however, with a bright smile.

"It isn't so nice to-day, is it?" she called blithesomely. "I'm glad it doesn't rain always, anyhow!"

The man did not even grunt this time, nor turn his head. Pollyanna decided that of course he did not hear her. The next time, therefore (which happened to be the following day), she spoke up louder. She thought it particularly necessary to do this, anyway, for the Man was striding along, his hands behind his back, and his eyes on the ground--which seemed, to Pollyanna, preposterous in the face of the glorious sunshine and the freshly-washed morning air: Pollyanna, as a special treat, was on a morning errand to-day.

"How do you do?" she chirped. "I'm so glad it isn't yesterday, aren't you?

The man stopped abruptly. There was an angry scowl on his face.

"See here, little girl, we might just as well settle this thing right now, once for all," he began testily. "I've got something besides the weather to think of. I don't know whether the sun shines or not." Pollyanna beamed joyously.

"No, sir; I thought you didn't. That's why I told you."

"Yes; well--Eh? What?" he broke off sharply, in sudden understanding of her words.

As spring came on, a new set of amusements became the fashion, and the lengthening days gave long afternoons for work and play of all sorts. The garden had to be put in order, and each sister had a quarter of the little plot to do what she liked with. Hannah used to say, "I'd know which each of them gardings belonged to, ef I see 'em in Chiny," and so she might, for the girls' tastes differed as much as their characters. Meg's had roses and heliotrope, myrtle, and a little orange tree in it. Jo's bed was never alike two seasons, for she was always trying experiments. This year it was to be a plantation of sun flowers, the seeds of which cheerful land aspiring plant were to feed Aunt Cockle-top and her family of chicks. Beth had old-fashioned fragrant flowers in her garden, sweet peas and mignonette, larkspur, pinks, pansies, and southernwood, with chickweed for the birds and catnip for the pussies. Amy had a bower in hers, rather small and earwiggy, but very pretty to look at, with honeysuckle and morning-glories hanging their colored horns and bells in graceful wreaths all over it, tall white lilies, delicate ferns, and as many brilliant, picturesque plants as would consent to blossom there.

Gardening, walks, rows on the river, and flower hunts employed the fine days, and for rainy ones, they had house diversions, some old, some new, all more or less original. One of these was the `P.C', for as secret societies were the fashion, it was thought proper to have one, and as all of the girls admired Dickens, they called themselves the Pickwick Club. With a few interruptions, they had kept this up for a year, and met every Saturday evening in the big garret, on which occasions the ceremonies were as follows: Three chairs were arranged in a row before a table on which was a lamp, also four white badges, with a big `P.C.' in different colors on each, and the weekly newspaper called, The Pickwick Portfolio, to which all contributed something, while Jo, who reveled in pens and ink, was the editor. At seven o'clock, the four members ascended to the clubroom, tied their badges round their heads, and took their seats with great solemnity. Meg, as the eldest, was Samuel Pickwick, Jo, being of a literary turn, Augustus Snodgrass, Beth, because she was round and rosy, Tracy Tupman, and Amy, who was always trying to do what she couldn't, was Nathaniel Winkle. Pickwick, the president, read the paper, which was filled with original tales, poetry, local news, funny advertisements, and hints, in which they good-naturedly reminded each other of their faults and short comings. On one occasion, Mr. Pickwick put on a pair of spectacles without any glass, rapped upon the table, hemmed, and having stared hard at Mr. Snodgrass, who was tilting back in his chair, till he arranged himself

I cannot feel that I have done my duty as humble historian of the March family, without devoting at least one chapter to the two most precious and important members of it. Daisy and Demi had now arrived at years of discretion, for in this fast age babies of three or four assert their rights, and get them, too, which is more than many of their elders do. If there ever were a pair of twins in danger of being utterly spoiled by adoration, it was these prattling Brookes. Of course they were the most remarkable children ever born, as will be shown when I mention that they walked at eight months, talked fluently at twelve months, and at two years they took their places at table, and behaved with a propriety which charmed all beholders. At three, Daisy demanded a `needler', and actually made a bag with four stitches in it. She likewise set up housekeeping in the sideboard, and managed a microscopic cooking stove with a skill that brought tears of pride to Hannah's eyes, while Demi learned his letters with his grandfather, who invented a new mode of teaching the alphabet by forming letters with his arms and legs, thus uniting gymnastics for head and heels. The boy early developed a mechanical genius which delighted his father and distracted his mother, for he tried to imitate every machine he saw, and kept the nursery in a chaotic condition, with his `sewinsheen', a mysterious structure of string, chairs, clothespins, and spools, for wheels to go `wound and wound'. Also a basket hung over the back of a chair, in which he vainly tried to hoist his too confiding sister, who, with feminine devotion, allowed her little head to be bumped till rescued, when the young inventor indignantly remarked, "Why, Marmar, dat's my lellywaiter, and me's trying to pull her up."

Though utterly unlike in character, the twins got on remarkably well together, and seldom quarreled more than thrice a day. Of course, Demi tyrannized over Daisy, and gallantly defended her from every other aggressor, while Daisy made a galley slave of herself, and adored her brother as the one perfect being in the world. A rosy, chubby, sunshiny little soul was Daisy, who found her way to everybody's heart, and nestled there. One of the captivating children, who seem made to be kissed and cuddled, adorned and adored like little goddesses, and produced for general

He acquitted his task with characteristic serenity, and invariably replied to the remonstrances of his fair companion, who was confused by his patience and generosity:

"It is in the interest of my journey--a part of my programme."

The purchases made, they returned to the hotel, where they dined at a sumptuously served table-d'hote; after which Aouda, shaking hands with her protector after the English fashion, retired to her room for rest. Mr. Fogg absorbed himself throughout the evening in the perusal of The Times and Illustrated London News.

Had he been capable of being astonished at anything, it would have been not to see his servant return at bedtime. But, knowing that the steamer was not to leave for Yokohama until the next morning, he did not disturb himself about the matter. When Passepartout did not appear the next morning to answer his master's bell, Mr. Fogg, not betraying the least vexation, contented himself with taking his carpet-bag, calling Aouda, and sending for a palanquin.

It was then eight o'clock; at half-past nine, it being then high tide, the Carnatic would leave the harbour. Mr. Fogg and Aouda got into the palanquin, their luggage being brought after on a wheelbarrow, and half an hour later stepped upon the quay whence they were to embark. Mr. Fogg then learned that the Carnatic had sailed the evening before. He had expected to find not only the steamer, but his domestic, and was forced to give up both; but no sign of disappointment appeared on his face, and he merely remarked to Aouda, "It is an accident, madam; nothing more."

At this moment a man who had been observing him attentively approached. It was Fix, who, bowing, addressed Mr. Fogg: "Were you not, like me, sir, a passenger by the Rangoon, which arrived yesterday?"

"I was, sir," replied Mr. Fogg coldly. "But I have not the honour--"

"Pardon me; I thought I should find your servant here."

"Do you know where he is, sir?" asked Aouda anxiously.

"What!" responded Fix, feigning surprise. "Is he not with you?"

"No," said Aouda. "He has not made his appearance since yesterday. Could he have gone on board the Carnatic without us?"

"Without you, madam?" answered the detective. "Excuse me, did you intend to sail in the Carnatic?"

"Yes, sir."

"So did I, madam, and I am excessively disappointed. The Carnatic, its repairs being completed, left Hong Kong twelve hours before the stated time, without any notice being given; and we must now wait a week for another steamer."

As he said "a week" Fix felt his heart leap for joy. Fogg detained at Hong Kong for a week! There would be time for the warrant to arrive, and fortune at last favoured the representative of the law. His horror may be imagined when he heard Mr. Fogg say, in his placid voice, "But there are other vessels besides the Carnatic, it seems to me, in the harbour of Hong Kong."

And, offering his arm to Aouda, he directed his steps toward the docks in search of some craft about to start. Fix, stupefied, followed; it seemed as if he were attached to Mr. Fogg by an invisible thread. Chance, however, appeared really to have abandoned the man it had hitherto served so well. For three hours Phileas Fogg wandered about the docks, with the determination, if necessary, to charter a vessel to carry him to Yokohama; but he could only find vessels which were loading or unloading, and which could not therefore set sail. Fix began to hope again.

But Mr. Fogg, far from being discouraged, was continuing his search, resolved not to stop if he had to resort to Macao, when he was accosted by a sailor on one of the wharves.

Chapter VI

IN WHICH FIX, THE DETECTIVE, BETRAYS A VERY NATURAL IMPATIENCE

The circumstances under which this telegraphic dispatch about Phileas Fogg was sent were as follows:

The steamer Mongolia, belonging to the Peninsular and Oriental Company, built of iron, of two thousand eight hundred tons burden, and five hundred horse-power, was due at eleven o'clock a.m. on Wednesday, the 9th of October, at Suez. The Mongolia plied regularly between Brindisi and Bombay via the Suez Canal, and was one of the fastest steamers belonging to the company, always making more than ten knots an hour between Brindisi and Suez, and nine and a half between Suez and Bombay.

Two men were promenading up and down the wharves, among the crowd of natives and strangers who were sojourning at this once straggling village-- now, thanks to the enterprise of M. Lesseps, a fast-growing town. One was the British consul at Suez, who, despite the prophecies of the English Government, and the unfavourable predictions of Stephenson, was in the habit of seeing, from his office window, English ships daily passing to and fro on the great canal, by which the old roundabout route from England to India by the Cape of Good Hope was abridged by at least a half. The other was a small, slight-built personage, with a nervous, intelligent face, and bright eyes peering out from under eyebrows which he was incessantly twitching. He was just now manifesting unmistakable signs of impatience, nervously pacing up and down, and unable to stand still for a moment. This was Fix, one of the detectives who had been dispatched from England in search of the bank robber; it was his task to narrowly watch every passenger who arrived at Suez, and to follow up all who seemed to be suspicious characters, or bore a resemblance

Chapter XIV

A YOUNG RAJAH

The moor was hidden in mist when the morning came, and the rain had not stopped pouring down. There could be no going out of doors. Martha was so busy that Mary had no opportunity of talking to her, but in the afternoon she asked her to come and sit with her in the nursery. She came bringing the stocking she was always knitting when she was doing nothing else.

"What's the matter with thee?" she asked as soon as they sat down. "Tha' looks as if tha'd somethin' to say."

"I have. I have found out what the crying was," said Mary.

Martha let her knitting drop on her knee and gazed at her with startled eyes.

"Tha' hasn't!" she exclaimed. "Never!"

"I heard it in the night," Mary went on. "And I got up and went to see where it came from. It was Colin. I found him."

Martha's face became red with fright.

"Eh! Miss Mary!" she said half crying. "Tha' shouldn't have done it--tha' shouldn't! Tha'll get me in trouble. I never told thee nothin' about him--but tha'll get me in trouble. I shall lose my place and what'll mother do!"

"You won't lose your place," said Mary. "He was glad I came. We talked and talked and he said he was glad I came."

Then came the horses. Having four feet, these managed rather better than the foot-soldiers: but even THEY stumbled now and then; and it seemed to be a regular rule that, whenever a horse stumbled the rider fell off instantly. The confusion got worse every moment, and Alice was very glad to get out of the wood into an open place, where she found the White King seated on the ground, busily writing in his memorandum-book.

`I've sent them all!' the King cried in a tone of delight, on seeing Alice. `Did you happen to meet any soldiers, my dear, as you came through the wood?'

`Yes, I did,' said Alice: `several thousand, I should think.'

`Four thousand two hundred and seven, that's the exact number,' the King said, referring to his book. `I couldn't send all the horses, you know, because two of them are wanted in the game. And I haven't sent the two Messengers, either. They're both gone to the town. Just look along the road, and tell me if you can see either of them.'

`I see nobody on the road,' said Alice.

`I only wish *I* had such eyes,' the King remarked in a fretful tone. `To be able to see Nobody! And at that distance, too! Why, it's as much as *I* can do to see real people, by this light!'

All this was lost on Alice, who was still looking intently along the road, shading her eyes with one hand. `I see somebody now!' she exclaimed at last. `But he's coming very slowly--and what curious attitudes he goes into!' (For the messenger kept skipping up and down, and wriggling like an eel, as he came along, with his great hands spread out like fans on each side.)

`Not at all,' said the King. `He's an Anglo-Saxon Messenger-- and those are Anglo-Saxon attitudes. He only does them when he's happy. His name is Haigha.' (He pronounced it so as to rhyme with `mayor.')

`I love my love with an H,' Alice couldn't help beginning, `because he is Happy. I hate him with an H, because he is Hideous. I fed him with--with--with Ham-sandwiches and Hay. His name is Haigha, and he lives--'

`He lives on the Hill,' the King remarked simply, without the least idea that he was joining in the game, while Alice was still hesitating for the name of a town beginning with H. `The other Messenger's called Hatta. I must have TWO, you know--to come and go. Once to come, and one to go.'

`I beg your pardon?' said Alice.

`It isn't respectable to beg,' said the King.

`I only meant that I didn't understand,' said Alice. `Why one to come and one to go?'

`Didn't I tell you?' the King repeated impatiently. `I must have Two--to fetch and carry. One to fetch, and one to carry.'

At this moment the Messenger arrived: he was far too much out of breath to say a word, and could only wave his hands about, and make the most fearful faces at the poor King.

`This young lady loves you with an H,' the King said, introducing Alice in the hope of turning off the Messenger's attention from himself--but it was no use--the Anglo-Saxon attitudes only got more extraordinary every moment, while the great eyes rolled wildly from side to side.

`You alarm me!' said the King. `I feel faint--Give me a ham sandwich!'

On which the Messenger, to Alice's great amusement, opened a bag that hung round his neck, and handed a sandwich to the King, who devoured it greedily.

`Another sandwich!' said the King.

`There's nothing but hay left now,' the Messenger said, peeping into the bag.

`Hay, then,' the King murmured in a faint whisper.

Alice was glad to see that it revived him a good deal. `There's nothing like eating hay when you're faint,' he remarked to her, as he munched away.

`Within the big valves of the door--which were open and broken--we found, instead of the customary hall, a long gallery lit by many side windows. At the first glance I was reminded of a museum. The tiled floor was thick with dust, and a remarkable array of miscellaneous objects was shrouded in the same grey covering. Then I perceived, standing strange and gaunt in the centre of the hall, what was clearly the lower part of a huge skeleton. I recognized by the oblique feet that it was some extinct creature after the fashion of the Megatherium. The skull and the upper bones lay beside it in the thick dust, and in one place, where rain-water had dropped through a leak in the roof, the thing itself had been worn away. Further in the gallery was the huge skeleton barrel of a Brontosaurus. My museum hypothesis was confirmed. Going towards the side I found what appeared to be sloping shelves, and clearing away the thick dust, I found the old familiar glass cases of our own time. But they must have been air-tight to judge from the fair preservation of some of their contents.

`Clearly we stood among the ruins of some latter-day South Kensington! Here, apparently, was the Palaeontological Section, and a very splendid array of fossils it must have been, though the inevitable process of decay that had been staved off for a time, and had, through the extinction of bacteria and fungi, lost ninety-nine hundredths of its force, was nevertheless, with extreme sureness if with extreme slowness at work again upon all its treasures. Here and there I found traces of the little people in the shape of rare fossils broken to pieces or threaded in strings upon reeds. And the cases had in some instances been bodily removed--by the Morlocks as I judged. The place was very silent. The thick dust deadened our footsteps. Weena, who had been rolling a sea urchin down the sloping glass of a case, presently came, as I stared about me, and very quietly took my hand and stood beside me.

`And at first I was so much surprised by this ancient monument of an intellectual age, that I gave no thought to the possibilities it presented. Even my preoccupation about the Time Machine receded a little from my mind.

`I am afraid I cannot convey the peculiar sensations of time travelling. They are excessively unpleasant. There is a feeling exactly like that one has upon a switchback--of a helpless headlong motion! I felt the same horrible anticipation, too, of an imminent smash. As I put on pace, night followed day like the flapping of a black wing. The dim suggestion of the laboratory seemed presently to fall away from me, and I saw the sun hopping swiftly across the sky, leaping it every minute, and every minute marking a day. I supposed the laboratory had been destroyed and I had come into the open air. I had a dim impression of scaffolding, but I was already going too fast to be conscious of any moving things. The slowest snail that ever crawled dashed by too fast for me. The twinkling succession of darkness and light was excessively painful to the eye. Then, in the intermittent darknesses, I saw the moon spinning swiftly through her quarters from new to full, and had a faint glimpse of the circling stars. Presently, as I went on, still gaining velocity, the palpitation of night and day merged into one continuous greyness; the sky took on a wonderful deepness of blue, a splendid luminous color like that of early twilight; the jerking sun became a streak of fire, a brilliant arch, in space; the moon a fainter fluctuating band; and I could see nothing of the stars, save now and then a brighter circle flickering in the blue.

`The landscape was misty and vague. I was still on the hill-side upon which this house now stands, and the shoulder rose above me grey and dim. I saw trees growing and changing like puffs of vapour, now brown, now green; they grew, spread, shivered, and passed away. I saw huge buildings rise up faint and fair, and pass like dreams. The whole surface of the earth seemed changed--melting and flowing under my eyes. The little hands upon the dials that registered my speed raced round faster and faster. Presently I noted that the sun belt swayed up and down, from solstice to solstice, in a minute or less, and that consequently my pace was over a year a minute; and minute by minute the white snow flashed across the world, and vanished, and was followed by the bright, brief green of spring.

Adeimantus said: 'Suppose a person to argue, Socrates, that you make your citizens miserable, and this by their own free-will; they are the lords of the city, and yet instead of having, like other men, lands and houses and money of their own, they live as mercenaries and are always mounting guard.' You may add, I replied, that they receive no pay but only their food, and have no money to spend on a journey or a mistress. 'Well, and what answer do you give?' My answer is, that our guardians may or may not be the happiest of men,--I should not be surprised to find in the long- run that they were,--but this is not the aim of our constitution, which was designed for the good of the whole and not of any one part. If I went to a sculptor and blamed him for having painted the eye, which is the noblest feature of the face, not purple but black, he would reply: 'The eye must be an eye, and you should look at the statue as a whole.' 'Now I can well imagine a fool's paradise, in which everybody is eating and drinking, clothed in purple and fine linen, and potters lie on sofas and have their wheel at hand, that they may work a little when they please; and cobblers and all the other classes of a State lose their distinctive character. And a State may get on without cobblers; but when the guardians degenerate into boon companions, then the ruin is complete. Remember that we are not talking of peasants keeping holiday, but of a State in which every man is expected to do his own work. The happiness resides not in this or that class, but in the State as a whole. I have another remark to make:--A middle condition is best for artisans; they should have money enough to buy tools, and not enough to be independent of business. And will not the same condition be best for our citizens? If they are poor, they will be mean; if rich, luxurious and lazy; and in neither case contented. 'But then how will our poor city be able to go to war against an enemy who has money?' There may be

a difficulty in fighting against one enemy; against two there will be none. In the first place, the contest will be carried on by trained warriors against well-to-do citizens: and is not a regular athlete an easy match for two stout opponents at least? Suppose also, that before engaging we send ambassadors to one of the two cities, saying, 'Silver and gold we have not; do you help us and take our share of the spoil;'--who would fight against the lean, wiry dogs, when they might join with them in preying upon the fatted sheep? 'But if many states join their resources, shall we not be in danger?' I am amused to hear you use the word 'state' of any but our own State. They are 'states,' but not 'a state'--many in one. For in every state there are two hostile nations, rich and poor, which you may set one against the other. But our State, while she remains true to her principles, will be in very deed the mightiest of Hellenic states.

To the size of the state there is no limit but the necessity of unity; it must be neither too large nor too small to be one. This is a matter of secondary importance, like the principle of transposition which was intimated in the parable of the earthborn men. The meaning there implied was that every man should do that for which he was fitted, and be at one with himself, and then the whole city would be united. But all these things are secondary, if education, which is the great matter, be duly regarded. When the wheel has once been set in motion, the speed is always increasing; and each generation improves upon the preceding, both in physical and moral qualities. The care of the governors should be directed to preserve music and gymnastic from innovation; alter the songs of a country, Damon says, and you will soon end by altering its laws. The change appears innocent at first, and begins in play; but the evil soon becomes serious,

In Westminster Hall I found nobody; not even the crowd of crawling varlets, who used to be craving evermore for employment or for payment. I knocked at three doors, one after other, of lobbies going out of it, where I had formerly seen some officers and people pressing in and out, but for my trouble I took nothing, except some thumps from echo. And at last an old man told me that all the lawyers were gone to see the result of their own works, in the fields of Lincoln's Inn.

However, in a few days' time, I had better fortune; for the court was sitting and full of business, to clear off the arrears of work, before the lawyers' holiday. As I was waiting in the hall for a good occasion, a man with horsehair on his head, and a long blue bag in his left hand, touched me gently on the arm, and led me into a quiet place. I followed him very gladly, being confident that he came to me with a message from the Justiciaries. But after taking pains to be sure that none could overhear us, he turned on me suddenly, and asked,--

'Now, John, how is your dear mother?'

'Worshipful sir' I answered him, after recovering from my surprise at his knowledge of our affairs, and kindly interest in them, 'it is two months now since I have seen her. Would to God that I only knew how she is faring now, and how the business of the farm goes!'

'Sir, I respect and admire you,' the old gentleman replied, with a bow very low and genteel; 'few young court-gallants of our time are so reverent and dutiful. Oh, how I did love my mother!' Here he turned up his eyes to heaven, in a

And thereupon I struck aside; not liking to run away quite, as some people might call it; but seeking to look like a wanderer who was come to see the valley, and had seen almost enough of it. Herein I should have succeeded, and gone home, and then been angry at my want of courage, but that on the very turn and bending of my footsteps, the woman in the distance lifted up her staff to me, so that I was bound to stop.

And now, being brought face to face, by the will of God (as one might say) with anything that might come of it, I kept myself quite straight and stiff, and thrust away all white feather, trusting in my Bible still, hoping that it would protect me, though I had disobeyed it. But upon that remembrance, my conscience took me by the leg, so that I could not go forward.

All this while, the fearful woman was coming near and more near to me; and I was glad to sit down on a rock because my knees were shaking so. I tried to think of many things, but none of them would come to me; and I could not take my eyes away, though I prayed God to be near me.

But when she was come so nigh to me that I could descry her features, there was something in her countenance that made me not dislike her. She looked as if she had been visited by many troubles, and had felt them one by one, yet held enough of kindly nature still to grieve for others. Long white hair, on either side, was falling down below her chin; and through her wrinkles clear bright eyes seemed to spread themselves upon me. Though I had plenty of time to think, I was taken by surprise no less, and unable to say anything; yet eager to hear the silence broken, and longing for a noise or two.

Chapter 23

Mr. Pocket said he was glad to see me, and he hoped I was not sorry to see him. "For, I really am not," he added, with his son's smile, "an alarming personage." He was a young-looking man, in spite of his perplexities and his very grey hair, and his manner seemed quite natural. I use the word natural, in the sense of its being unaffected; there was something comic in his distraught way, as though it would have been downright ludicrous but for his own perception that it was very near being so. When he had talked with me a little, he said to Mrs. Pocket, with a rather anxious contraction of his eyebrows, which were black and handsome, "Belinda, I hope you have welcomed Mr. Pip?" And she looked up from her book, and said, "Yes." She then smiled upon me in an absent state of mind, and asked me if I liked the taste of orange-flower water? As the question had no bearing, near or remote, on any foregone or subsequent transaction, I consider it to have been thrown out, like her previous approaches, in general conversational condescension.

I found out within a few hours, and may mention at once, that Mrs. Pocket was the only daughter of a certain quite accidental deceased Knight, who had invented for himself a conviction that his deceased father would have been made a Baronet but for somebody's determined opposition arising out of entirely personal motives - I forget whose, if I ever knew - the Sovereign's, the Prime Minister's, the Lord

"Yes, to be sure," said Wemmick. "Of course there can be no objection to your being sorry for him, and I'd put down a five-pound note myself to get him out of it. But what I look at, is this. The late Compeyson having been beforehand with him in intelligence of his return, and being so determined to bring him to book, I do not think he could have been saved. Whereas, the portable property certainly could have been saved. That's the difference between the property and the owner, don't you see?"

I invited Wemmick to come up-stairs, and refresh himself with a glass of grog before walking to Walworth. He accepted the invitation. While he was drinking his moderate allowance, he said, with nothing to lead up to it, and after having appeared rather fidgety:

"What do you think of my meaning to take a holiday on Monday, Mr. Pip?"

"Why, I suppose you have not done such a thing these twelve months."

"These twelve years, more likely," said Wemmick. "Yes. I'm going to take a holiday. More than that; I'm going to take a walk. More than that; I'm going to ask you to take a walk with me."

I was about to excuse myself, as being but a bad companion just than, when Wemmick anticipated me.

"I know your engagements," said he, "and I know you are out of sorts, Mr. Pip. But if you could oblige me, I should take it as a kindness. It ain't a long walk, and it's an early one. Say it might occupy you (including breakfast on the walk) from eight to twelve. Couldn't you stretch a point and manage it?"

He had done so much for me at various times, that this was very little to do for him. I said I could manage it - would manage it - and he was so very much pleased by my acquiescence, that I was pleased too. At his particular request, I appointed to call for him at

As watching is best done invisibly, she usually carried a dark lantern in her hand, and every now and then turned on the light to examine nooks and corners with the coolness of a metropolitan policeman. This coolness may have owed its existence not so much to her fearlessness of expected danger as to her freedom from the suspicion of any; her worst anticipated discovery being that a horse might not be well bedded, the fowls not all in, or a door not closed.

This night the buildings were inspected as usual, and she went round to the farm paddock. Here the only sounds disturbing the stillness were steady munchings of many mouths, and stentorian breathings from all but invisible noses, ending in snores and puffs like the blowing of bellows slowly. Then the munching would recommence, when the lively imagination might assist the eye to discern a group of pink-white nostrils, shaped as caverns, and very clammy and humid on their surfaces, not exactly pleasant to the touch until one got used to them; the mouths beneath having a great partiality for closing upon any loose end of Bathsheba's apparel which came within reach of their tongues. Above each of these a still keener vision suggested a brown forehead and two staring though not unfriendly eyes, and above all a pair of whitish crescent- shaped horns like two particularly new moons, an occasional stolid "moo!" proclaiming beyond the shade of a doubt that these phenomena were the features and persons of Daisy, Whitefoot, Bonny-lass, Jolly-O, Spot, Twinkle-eye, etc., etc. -- the respectable dairy of Devon cows belonging to Bathsheba aforesaid.

Her way back to the house was by a path through a young plantation of tapering firs, which had been planted some years earlier to shelter the premises from the north wind. By reason of the density of the interwoven foliage overhead, it was gloomy there at cloudless noontide, twilight in the evening, dark as midnight at dusk, and black as the ninth plague of Egypt at midnight. To describe the spot is to call it a vast, low, naturally formed hall, the plumy ceiling of which was supported by slender pillars of living wood, the floor being covered with a soft dun carpet of dead spikelets and mildewed cones, with a tuft of grass-blades here and there.

EFFECT OF THE LETTER -- SUNRISE

AT dusk, on the evening of St. Valentine's Day, Bold-wood sat down to supper as usual, by a beaming fire of aged logs. Upon the mantel-shelf before him was a time-piece, surmounted by a spread eagle, and upon the eagle's wings was the letter Bathsheba had sent. Here the bachelor's gaze was continually fastening itself, till the large red seal became as a blot of blood on the retina of his eye; and as he ate and drank he still read in fancy the words thereon, although they were too remote for his sight --

"MARRY ME."

The pert injunction was like those crystal substances which, colourless themselves, assume the tone of objects about them. Here, in the quiet of Boldwood's parlour, where everything that was not grave was extraneous, and where the atmosphere was that of a Puritan Sunday lasting all the week, the letter and its dictum changed their tenor from the thoughtlessness of their origin to a deep solemnity, imbibed from their accessories now.

Since the receipt of the missive in the morning, Boldwood had felt the symmetry of his existence to be slowly getting distorted in the direction of an ideal passion. The disturbance was as the first floating weed to Columbus -- the contemptibly little suggesting possibilities of the infinitely great.

The letter must have had an origin and a motive. That the latter was of the smallest magnitude compatible with its existence at all, Boldwood, of course, did not know. And such an explanation did not strike him as a possibility even. It is foreign to a mystified condition of mind to realize of the mystifier that the processes of approving a course suggested by circumstance, and of striking out a course from inner impulse, would look the same in the result. The vast difference between starting a train of events, and directing into a particular groove a series already started, is rarely apparent to the person confounded by the issue.

When Boldwood went to bed he placed the valentine in the corner of the looking-glass. He was conscious of its presence, even when his back was turned upon it. It was the first time in Boldwood's life that such an event had occurred. The same fascination that caused him to think it an act which

Awaking in the middle of a prodigiously tough snore, and sitting up in bed to get his thoughts together, Scrooge had no occasion to be told that the bell was again upon the stroke of One. He felt that he was restored to consciousness in the right nick of time, for the especial purpose of holding a conference with the second messenger despatched to him through Jacob Marley's intervention. But, finding that he turned uncomfortably cold when he began to wonder which of his curtains this new spectre would draw back, he put them every one aside with his own hands, and lying down again, established a sharp look-out all round the bed. For, he wished to challenge the Spirit on the moment of its appearance, and did not wish to be taken by surprise, and made nervous.

Gentlemen of the free-and-easy sort, who plume themselves on being acquainted with a move or two, and being usually equal to the time-of-day, express the wide range of their capacity for adventure by observing that they are good for anything from pitch-and-toss to manslaughter; between which opposite extremes, no doubt, there lies a tolerably wide and comprehensive range of subjects. Without venturing for Scrooge quite as hardily as this, I don't mind calling on you to believe that he was ready for a good broad field of strange appearances, and that nothing between a baby and rhinoceros would have astonished him very much.

Now, being prepared for almost anything, he was not by any means prepared for nothing; and, consequently, when the Bell struck One, and no shape appeared, he was taken with a violent fit of trembling. Five minutes, ten minutes, a quarter of an hour went by, yet nothing came. All this time, he lay upon his bed, the very core and centre of a blaze of ruddy light, which streamed upon it when the clock proclaimed the hour; and which, being only light, was more alarming than a dozen ghosts, as he was powerless to make out what it meant, or would be at; and was sometimes apprehensive that he might be at that very moment an interesting case of spontaneous combustion, without having the consolation of knowing it. At last, however, he began to think -- as you or I would have thought at first; for it is always the person not in the predicament who knows what ought to have been done in it, and would unquestionably have done it too -- at last, I say, he began to think that the source and secret of this ghostly

The idea being an alarming one, he scrambled out of bed, and groped his way to the window. He was obliged to rub the frost off with the sleeve of his dressing-gown before he could see anything; and could see very little then. All he could make out was, that it was still very foggy and extremely cold, and that there was no noise of people running to and fro, and making a great stir, as there unquestionably would have been if night had beaten off bright day, and taken possession of the world. This was a great relief, because "Three days after sight of this First of Exchange pay to Mr. Ebenezer Scrooge on his order," and so forth, would have become a mere United States security if there were no days to count by.

Scrooge went to bed again, and thought, and thought, and thought it over and over, and could make nothing of it. The more he thought, the more perplexed he was; and, the more he endeavoured not to think, the more he thought.

Marley's Ghost bothered him exceedingly. Every time he resolved within himself, after mature inquiry that it was all a dream, his mind flew back again, like a strong spring released, to its first position, andpresented the same problem to be worked all through, "Was it a dream or not?"

Scrooge lay in this state until the chime had gone three-quarters more, when he remembered, on a sudden, that the Ghost hadwarned him of a visitation when the bell tolled one. He resolved to lie awake until the hour
was passed; and, considering that he could no more go to sleep than go to heaven, this was, perhaps, the wisest resolution in his power.

The quarter was so long, that he was more than once convinced he must have sunk into a doze unconsciously, and missed the clock. At length it broke upon his listening ear.

"Ding, dong!"

"A quarter past," said Scrooge, counting.

"Ding, dong!"

"I don't often speak of myself," said John, "but as you are going away from us out into the world to shift for yourself I'll just tell you how I look on these things. I was just as old as Joseph when my father and mother died of the fever within ten days of each other, and left me and my cripple sister Nelly alone in the world, without a relation that we could look to for help. I was a farmer's boy, not earning enough to keep myself, much less both of us, and she must have gone to the workhouse but for our mistress (Nelly calls her her angel, and she has good right to do so). She went and hired a room for her with old Widow Mallet, and she gave her knitting and needlework when she was able to do it; and when she was ill she sent her dinners and many nice, comfortable things, and was like a mother to her. Then the master he took me into the stable under old Norman, the coachman that was then. I had my food at the house and my bed in the loft, and a suit of clothes, and three shillings a week, so that I could help Nelly. Then there was Norman; he might have turned round and said at his age he could not be troubled with a raw boy from the plow-tail, but he was like a father to me, and took no end of pains with me. When the old man died some years after I stepped into his place, and now of course I have top wages, and can lay by for a rainy day or a sunny day, as it may happen, and Nelly is as happy as a bird. So you see, James, I am not the man that should turn up his nose at a little boy and vex a good, kind master. No, no! I shall miss you very much, James, but we shall pull through, and there's nothing like doing a kindness when 'tis put in your way, and I am glad I can do it."

"Then," said James, "you don't hold with that saying, `Everybody look after himself, and take care of number one'?"

"No, indeed," said John, "where should I and Nelly have been if master and mistress and old Norman had only taken care of number one? Why, she in the workhouse and I hoeing turnips! Where would Black Beauty and Ginger have been if you had only thought of number one? why, roasted to death! No, Jim, no! that is a selfish, heathenish saying, whoever uses it; and any man who thinks he has nothing to do but take care of number one, why, it's a pity but what he had been drowned like a puppy or a kitten, before he got his eyes open; that's what I think," said John, with a very decided jerk of his head.

James laughed at this; but there was a thickness in his voice when he said, "You have been my best friend except my mother; I hope you won't forget me."

The night before the 'Pennsylvania' left, Henry and I sat chatting on a freight pile on the levee till midnight. The subject of the chat, mainly, was one which I think we had not exploited before--steamboat disasters.One was then on its way to us, little as we suspected it; the water which was to make the steam which should cause it, was washing past some point fifteen hundred miles up the river while we talked;-- but it would arrive at the right time and the right place. We doubted if persons not clothed with authority were of much use in cases of disaster and attendant panic; still, they might be of SOME use; so we decided that if a disaster ever fell within our experience we would at least stick to the boat, and give such minor service as chance might throw in the way. Henry remembered this, afterward, when the disaster came, and acted accordingly.

The 'Lacey' started up the river two days behind the 'Pennsylvania.' We touched at Greenville, Mississippi, a couple of days out, and somebody shouted--

'The "Pennsylvania" is blown up at Ship Island, and a hundred and fifty lives lost!'

At Napoleon, Arkansas, the same evening, we got an extra, issued by a Memphis paper, which gave some particulars. It mentioned my brother, and said he was not hurt.

Further up the river we got a later extra.My brother was again mentioned; but this time as being hurt beyond help. We did not get full details of the catastrophe until we reached Memphis. This is the sorrowful story--

It was six o'clock on a hot summer morning. The 'Pennsylvania' was creeping along, north of Ship Island, about sixty miles below Memphis on a half-head of steam, towing a wood-flat which was fast being emptied. George Ealer was in the pilot-house-alone, I think; the second engineer and a striker had the watch in the engine room; the second mate had the watch on deck; George Black, Mr. Wood, and my brother, clerks, were asleep, as were also Brown

DURING this big rise these small-fry craft were an intolerable nuisance. We were running chute after chute,--a new world to me,--and if there was a particularly cramped place in a chute, we would be pretty sure to meet a broad-horn there; and if he failed to be there, we would find him in a still worse locality, namely, the head of the chute, on the shoal water. And then there would be no end of profane cordialities exchanged.

Sometimes, in the big river, when we would be feeling our way cautiously along through a fog, the deep hush would suddenly be broken by yells and a clamor of tin pans, and all in instant a log raft would appear vaguely through the webby veil, close upon us; and then we did not wait to swap knives, but snatched our engine bells out by the roots and piled on all the steam we had, to scramble out of the way! One doesn't hit a rock or a solid log craft with a steamboat when he can get excused.

You will hardly believe it, but many steamboat clerks always carried a large assortment of religious tracts with them in those old departed steamboating days.Indeed they did. Twenty times a day we would be cramping up around a bar, while a string of these small-fry rascals were drifting down into the head of the bend away above and beyond us a couple of miles. Now a skiff would dart away from one of them, and come fighting its laborious way across the desert of water. It would 'ease all,' in the shadow of our forecastle, and the panting oarsmen would shout, 'Gimme a pa-a-per!' as the skiff drifted swiftly astern. The clerk would throw over a file of New Orleans journals. If these were picked up without comment, you might notice that now a dozen other skiffs had been drifting down upon us without saying anything. You understand, they had been waiting to see how No. 1 was going to fare. No. 1 making no comment, all the rest would bend to their oars and come on, now; and as fast as they came the clerk would heave over neat bundles of religious tracts, tied to shingles. The amount of hard swearing which twelve packages of religious literature will command when impartially divided up among twelve raftsmen's crews, who have pulled a heavy skiff two miles on a hot day to get them, is simply incredible.

There is a tradition that Island 37 was one of the principal abiding places of the once celebrated 'Murel's Gang.'This was a colossal combination of robbers, horse-thieves, negro-stealers, and counterfeiters, engaged in business along the river some fifty or sixty years ago. While our journey across the country towards St. Louis was in progress we had had no end of Jesse James and his stirring history; for he had just been assassinated by an agent of the Governor of Missouri, and was in consequence occupying a good deal of space in the newspapers. Cheap histories of him were for sale by train boys. According to these, he was the most marvelous creature of his kind that had ever existed. It was a mistake.Murel was his equal in boldness; in pluck; in rapacity; in cruelty, brutality, heartlessness, treachery, and in general and comprehensive vileness and shamelessness; and very much his superior in some larger aspects.James was a retail rascal; Murel, wholesale. James's modest genius dreamed of no loftier flight than the planning of raids upon cars, coaches, and country banks; Murel projected negro insurrections and the capture of New Orleans; and furthermore, on occasion, this Murel could go into a pulpit and edify the congregation. What are James and his half-dozen vulgar rascals compared with this stately old-time criminal, with his sermons, his meditated insurrections and city-captures, and his majestic following of ten hundred men, sworn to do his evil will!

Here is a paragraph or two concerning this big operator, from a now forgotten book which was published half a century ago--

He appears to have been a most dexterous as well as consummate villain. When he traveled, his usual disguise was that of an itinerant preacher; and it is said that his discourses were very 'soul-moving'-- interesting the hearers so much that they forgot to look after their horses, which were carried away by his confederates while he was preaching. But the stealing of horses in one State, and selling them in another, was but a small portion of their business; the most lucrative was the enticing slaves to run away from their masters, that they might sell them in another quarter.This was arranged as follows; they would tell a negro that if he would run away from his master, and allow them to sell him, he should receive a portion of the money paid for him, and that upon his return to them a second time they would

LILY-BELL AND THISTLEDOWN.

ONCE upon a time, two little Fairies went out into the world, to seek their fortune. Thistle-down was as gay and gallant a little Elf as ever spread a wing. His purple mantle, and doublet of green, were embroidered with the brightest threads, and the plume in his cap came always from the wing of the gayest butterfly.

But he was not loved in Fairy-Land, for, like the flower whose name and colors he wore, though fair to look upon, many were the little thorns of cruelty and selfishness that lay concealed by his gay mantle. Many a gentle flower and harmless bird died by his hand, for he cared for himself alone, and whatever gave him pleasure must be his, though happy hearts were rendered sad, and peaceful homes destroyed.

Such was Thistledown; but far different was his little friend, Lily-Bell. Kind, compassionate, and loving, wherever her gentle face was seen, joy and gratitude were found; no suffering flower or insect, that did not love and bless the kindly Fairy; and thus all Elf-Land looked upon her as a friend.

Nor did this make her vain and heedless of others; she humb]y dwelt among them, seeking to do all the good she might; and many a houseless bird and hungry insect that Thistledown had harmed did she feed and shelter, and in return no evil could befall her, for so many friends were all about her, seeking to repay her tenderness and love by their watchful care.

She would not now have left Fairy-Land, but to help and counsel her wild companion, Thistledown, who, discontented with his quiet home, WOULD seek his fortune in the great world, and she feared he would suffer from his own faults for others would not always be as gentle and forgiving as his kindred. So the kind little Fairy left her home and friends to go with him; and thus, side by side, they flew beneath the bright summer sky.

As thus she spoke, the Elf took from her bosom a graceful flower, whose snow-white leaves shone with a strange, soft light. "This is a fairy flower," said the Elf, "invisible to every eye save yours; now listen while I tell its power, Annie. When your heart is filled with loving thoughts, when some kindly deed has been done, some duty well performed, then from the flower there will arise the sweetest, softest fragrance, to reward and gladden you. But when an unkind word is on your lips, when a selfish, angry feeling rises in your heart, or an unkind, cruel deed is to be done, then will you hear the soft, low chime of the flower-bell; listen to its warning, let the word remain unspoken, the deed undone, and in the quiet joy of your own heart, and the magic perfume of your bosom flower, you will find a sweet reward."

"O kind and generous Fairy, how can I ever thank you for this lovely gift!" cried Annie. "I will be true, and listen to my little bell whenever it may ring. But shall I never see YOU more? Ah! if you would only stay with me, I should indeed be good."

"I cannot stay now, little Annie," said the Elf, "but when another Spring comes round, I shall be here again, to see how well the fairy gift has done its work. And now farewell, dear child; be faithful to yourself, and the magic flower will never fade."

Then the gentle Fairy folded her little arms around Annie's neck, laid a soft kiss on her cheek, and, spreading wide her shining wings, flew singing up among the white clouds floating in the sky.

And little Annie sat among her flowers, and watched with wondering joy the fairy blossom shining on her breast.

The pleasant days of Spring and Summer passed away, and in little Annie's garden Autumn flowers were blooming everywhere, with each day's sun and dew growing still more beautiful and bright; but the fairy flower, that should have been the loveliest of all, hung pale and drooping on little Annie's bosom; its fragrance seemed quite gone, and the clear, low music of its warning chime rang often in her ear.

When first the Fairy placed it there, she had been pleased with her new gift, and for a while obeyed the fairy bell, and often tried to win some fragrance from the flower, by kind and pleasant words and actions; then, as the Fairy said, she found a sweet reward in the strange, soft perfume of the magic blossom, as it shone upon her breast; but selfish thoughts would come to

Murdstone and Grinby's warehouse was at the waterside. It was down in Blackfriars. Modern improvements have altered the place; but it was the last house at the bottom of a narrow street, curving down hill to the river, with some stairs at the end, where people took boat. It was a crazy old house with a wharf of its own, abutting on the water when the tide was in, and on the mud when the tide was out, and literally overrun with rats. Its panelled rooms, discoloured with the dirt and smoke of a hundred years, I dare say; its decaying floors and staircase; the squeaking and scuffling of the old grey rats down in the cellars; and the dirt and rottenness of the place; are things, not of many years ago, in my mind, but of the present instant. They are all before me, just as they were in the evil hour when I went among them for the first time, with my trembling hand in Mr. Quinion's.

Murdstone and Grinby's trade was among a good many kinds of people, but an important branch of it was the supply of wines and spirits to certain packet ships. I forget now where they chiefly went, but I think there were some among them that made voyages both to the East and West Indies. I know that a great many empty bottles were one of the consequences of this traffic, and that certain men and boys were employed to examine them against the light, and reject those that were flawed, and to rinse and wash them. When the empty bottles ran short, there were labels to be pasted on full ones, or corks to be fitted to them, or seals to be put upon the corks, or finished bottles to be packed in casks. All this work was my work, and of the boys employed upon it I was one.

There were three or four of us, counting me. My working place was established in a corner of the warehouse, where Mr. Quinion could see me, when he chose to stand up on the bottom rail of his stool in the counting-house, and look at me through a window above the desk. Hither, on the first morning of my so auspiciously beginning life on my own account, the oldest of the regular boys was summoned to show me my business. His name was Mick Walker, and he wore a ragged apron and a paper cap. He informed me that his father was a bargeman, and walked, in a black velvet head-dress, in the Lord Mayor's Show. He also informed me that our principal associate would be another boy whom he introduced by the - to me -

It has not occurred to me to mention Peggotty since I ran away; but, of course, I wrote her a letter almost as soon as I was housed at Dover, and another, and a longer letter, containing all particulars fully related, when my aunt took me formally under her protection. On my being settled at Doctor Strong's I wrote to her again, detailing my happy condition and prospects. I never could have derived anything like the pleasure from spending the money Mr. Dick had given me, that I felt in sending a gold half-guinea to Peggotty, per post, enclosed in this last letter, to discharge the sum I had borrowed of her: in which epistle, not before, I mentioned about the young man with the donkey-cart.

To these communications Peggotty replied as promptly, if not as concisely, as a merchant's clerk. Her utmost powers of expression (which were certainly not great in ink) were exhausted in the attempt to write what she felt on the subject of my journey. Four sides of incoherent and interjectional beginnings of sentences, that had no end, except blots, were inadequate to afford her any relief. But the blots were more expressive to me than the best composition; for they showed me that Peggotty had been crying all over the paper, and what could I have desired more?

I made out, without much difficulty, that she could not take quite kindly to my aunt yet. The notice was too short after so long a prepossession the other way. We never knew a person, she wrote; but to think that Miss Betsey should seem to be so different from what she had been thought to be, was a Moral! - that was her word. She was evidently still afraid of Miss Betsey, for she sent her grateful duty to her but timidly; and she was evidently afraid of me, too, and entertained the probability of my running away again soon: if I might judge from the repeated hints she threw out, that the coach-fare to Yarmouth was always to be had of her for the asking.

She gave me one piece of intelligence which affected me very much, namely, that there had been a sale of the furniture at our old home, and that Mr. and Miss Murdstone were gone away, and the house was shut up, to be let or sold. God knows I had no part in it

The appearance of the little sitting-room as they entered, was tranquillity itself; Mrs. Bates, deprived of her usual employment, slumbering on one side of the fire, Frank Churchill, at a table near her, most deedily occupied about her spectacles, and Jane Fairfax, standing with her back to them, intent on her pianoforte.

Busy as he was, however, the young man was yet able to shew a most happy countenance on seeing Emma again.

"This is a pleasure," said he, in rather a low voice, "coming at least ten minutes earlier than I had calculated. You find me trying to be useful; tell me if you think I shall succeed."

"What!" said Mrs. Weston, "have not you finished it yet? you would not earn a very good livelihood as a working silversmith at this rate."

"I have not been working uninterruptedly," he replied, "I have been assisting Miss Fairfax in trying to make her instrument stand steadily, it was not quite firm; an unevenness in the floor, I believe. You see we have been wedging one leg with paper. This was very kind of you to be persuaded to come. I was almost afraid you would be hurrying home."

He contrived that she should be seated by him; and was sufficiently employed in looking out the best baked apple for her, and trying to make her help or advise him in his work, till Jane Fairfax was quite ready to sit down to the pianoforte again. That she was not immediately ready, Emma did suspect to arise from the state of her nerves; she had not yet possessed the instrument long enough to touch it without emotion; she must reason herself into the power of performance; and Emma could not but pity such feelings, whatever their origin, and could not but resolve never to expose them to her neighbour again.At last Jane began, and though the first bars were feebly given, the powers of the

Mrs. Weston's friends were all made happy by her safety; and if the satisfaction of her well-doing could be increased to Emma, it was by knowing her to be the mother of a little girl. She had been decided in wishing for a Miss Weston. She would not acknowledge that it was with any view of making a match for her, hereafter, with either of Isabella's sons; but she was convinced that a daughter would suit both father and mother best. It would be a great comfort to Mr. Weston, as he grew older-- and even Mr. Weston might be growing older ten years hence--to have his fireside enlivened by the sports and the nonsense, the freaks and the fancies of a child never banished from home; and Mrs. Weston-- no one could doubt that a daughter would be most to her; and it would be quite a pity that any one who so well knew how to teach, should not have their powers in exercise again.

"She has had the advantage, you know, of practising on me," she continued--"like La Baronne d'Almane on La Comtesse d'Ostalis, in Madame de Genlis' Adelaide and Theodore, and we shall now see her own little Adelaide educated on a more perfect plan."

"That is," replied Mr. Knightley, "she will indulge her even more than she did you, and believe that she does not indulge her at all. It will be the only difference."

"Poor child!" cried Emma; "at that rate, what will become of her?"

"Nothing very bad.--The fate of thousands. She will be disagreeable in infancy, and correct herself as she grows older. I am losing all my bitterness against spoilt children, my dearest Emma. I, who am owing all my happiness to you, would not it be horrible ingratitude in me to be severe on them?"

Emma laughed, and replied: "But I had the assistance of all your endeavours to counteract the indulgence of other people. I doubt whether my own sense would have corrected me without it."

"Do you?--I have no doubt. Nature gave you understanding:-- Miss Taylor gave you principles. You must have done well. My

Made in the USA
Monee, IL
28 December 2023

50723857R00069